SAVING ENERGY

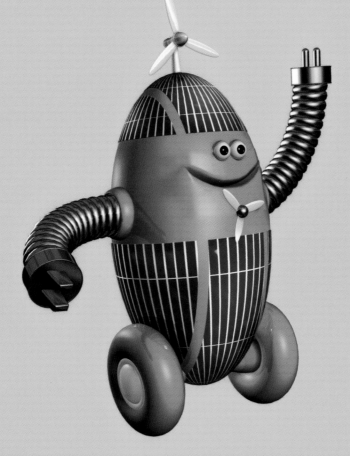

Neil Morris

QEB Publishing

Picture credits (t = top, b = bottom, l = left, r = right)

Corbis Tom & Dee Ann McCarthy 9b

Dreamstime 12t

Istockphoto 11, 13, 15, 19

Shutterstock Losevsky Pavel 2, Oguz Aral 4r, Viktor Gmyria 4l, pixelman 6t, Victoria Alexandrova 7, 8, Christopher Elwell 9t, Michaela Steininger 10, Dino Ablakovic 12b, Kevan O'Meara 14, Olga Vasilkova 16, 17, 18, Dainis Derics 20l, George Muresan 20r

Words in **bold** can be found in the glossary on page 22.

Published in the United States by
QEB Publishing, Inc.
3 Wrigley, Suite A
Irvine, CA 92618

www.qeb-publishing.com

Library of Congress Control Number: 2008010279

ISBN 978 1 59566 541 6

Printed and bound in China

Author Neil Morris
Consultant Bibi van der Zee
Editor Amanda Askew
Designer Elaine Wilkinson
Picture Researcher Maria Joannou
Illustrator Mark Turner for Beehive Illustration

Publisher Steve Evans
Creative Director Zeta Davies

Contents

What is energy?

▲ *A television works by using **electricity** to make the sound and picture.*

Energy from the Sun

Plant leaf

Water is taken in from the roots

Energy is the power that makes things move or work. Cars and buses are powered by **chemical** energy, such as gasoline or diesel **fuel**. Lights, computers, and televisions work by using electrical energy at the flick of a switch.

Did you know?

Plants use solar energy, or sunlight, to make food. Humans then eat plants–this is one way that we get energy for our bodies.

Oxygen gas is given off

All energy comes originally from the Earth's star, the Sun, which is like an enormous power plant. It sends us energy in sunbeams as heat and light. We turn this into energy that we can use.

Carbon dioxide gas is taken in

◀ Plants take in sunlight and use it with water and carbon dioxide to make their own sugary food. At the same time, they give off oxygen.

Why save energy?

It is important that we try to save as much energy as we can. We are using more coal, oil, and gas than ever before, and one day they will all run out.

▲ *Coal is a black or brown rock. It is taken from the ground by **mining**, then burned to make electricity.*

Did you know?

Coal, oil, and natural gas are called fossil fuels. They formed underground millions of years ago from the remains of prehistoric plants and animals.

When we burn fossil fuels in factories and cars, it causes **pollution**. This makes the air dirty, which damages our **environment**.

▲ Factories pump out waste gases as they burn fuel, such as coal. The gases make the air dirty.

Burning fuels

▲ A car is filled with fuel, such as gasoline. This burns inside the car, giving it the power to move.

We burn different forms of oil to power cars, trains, ships, and planes. In the home, gas can be burned to cook food and power central heating.

Coal and other fuels are used in **power stations** to make electricity. The fuels are burned, which creates heat. This is then used to boil water, which makes steam. The steam turns the wheel in a machine, which makes electricity.

▲ After making electricity, the hot air is cooled in large towers. The cooling towers give off steam.

You can do it

Find out how your friends get to school. Do they go by car or bus? Or do they save energy by walking or riding a bike? What about you?

Electric power

Power lines carry electricity from power stations to our neighborhood. Then cables take it to our homes, schools, and businesses. Electricity is instant energy. When we press a switch, there it is!

◄ Power lines are held up by big towers called pylons.

You can do it

What runs on electricity? Make a chart of the electrical items in the different rooms of your home.

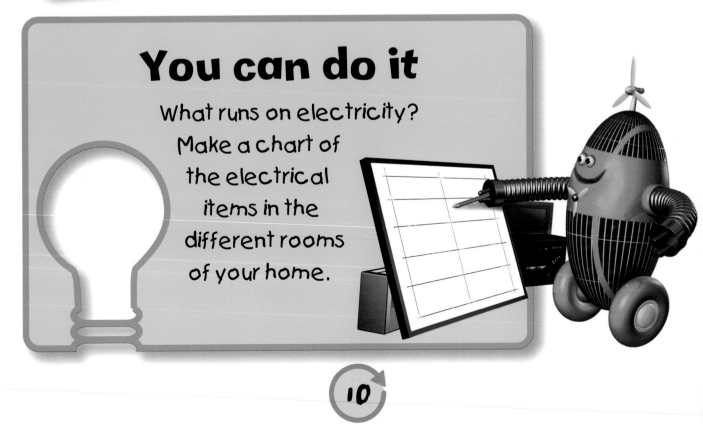

Batteries are small stores of energy. They provide power to make toys, flashlights, radios, and many other electrical items work. Some batteries can be **recharged** when they are empty and used again.

▲ These batteries have run out of power. They are put into a recharger, which is plugged into an electrical socket. This charges the batteries with electricity.

9V AA/AAA

Turn it off!

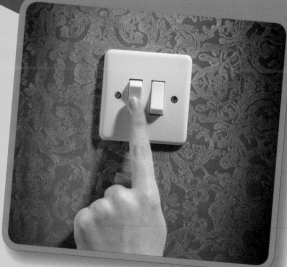

One of the best ways to save energy is to use less electricity at home. It is easy to turn electrical things off when we have finished with them.

▲ *Switching off lights when we are not using them saves a lot of energy.*

Equipment such as televisions often stay on standby when you switch them off with a remote control. They use a small amount of electricity because they are still on. This is a waste of energy.

▶ *Televisions should be switched off properly, instead of using a remote control to put them on standby. Turning off one television saves enough energy every day to power an energy-saving light bulb for six hours.*

Did you know?

Five energy-saving light bulbs use the same amount of electricity as one ordinary light bulb.

For electrical equipment that needs to be on for a lot of the time, energy can be saved by simply turning it down, rather than off. When it is cold, you could wear an extra sweater and turn the heating down a little.

▶ *Warm clothes can help us to save energy when heating our homes.*

Sun, wind, and water

▲ *In a wind farm, the blades of **turbines** turn with the force of the wind. This movement makes electricity.*

The energy of sunlight, wind, and water can be used to make electricity, too. Solar panels can capture the energy of the Sun. Wind can turn the blades of tall turbines. Huge walls, called dams, are built across rivers. Dams store water to make electricity.

◀ Many calculators are powered by a solar panel—the dark strip at the top. The panel needs to be in daylight for the calculator to work.

This kind of energy is called renewable, which means it will not run out. Solar panels are very useful for powering electrical appliances, such as calculators.

You can do it

Hang out washing on a clothes line to see how sunlight and wind dry clothes—without using any electricity!

Muscle power

When you walk or ride a bike, you use muscle power to move. This saves energy because you are not using fuel for a car or bus. It also causes less pollution in the environment.

◀ Riding a bike, walking, and running are good exercise.

You can do it

Draw a map of your neighborhood, showing where you can safely walk and ride. Where could there be more paths for pedestrians and cyclists?

Our muscles need their own source of energy, just like the rest of our body. All that energy comes from the food that we eat.

◀ *Food gives us energy. We need energy to make our muscles move.*

Energy in goods

Energy is needed to make things. For example, oil is used to make plastics, paints, tires, and other products. Energy is also used to power the machines that make the goods.

▲ *Energy is used to make paints, which may also contain oil.*

You can do it

Look on food packets at home or in the supermarket to see where your food comes from. Are the foods local, or have they been brought from far away?

It takes energy to take goods, including food, from one place to another. If we eat food that is grown locally, less energy is used to get the food to our stores.

▼ We can grow some of our own food, such as fruit and vegetables.

Wrapping up

◀ A thick layer of **insulation** in the outer walls of a house helps to keep it warm.

It takes energy to heat a building, and energy is wasted if we allow too much heat to escape. We can stop this from happening by using thick layers of material to insulate a house.

You can do it

Wrap bottles in tin foil, newspaper, and woolen socks. Fill the bottles with warm water and see which stay warm for the longest time.

◀ A hat, gloves, and coat are insulation for our bodies. They help to keep us warm on a cold day.

When we go out on a cold day, we wrap up by putting on extra clothes, such as a coat. This stops our bodies from losing too much heat.

Glossary

chemical   a substance made by mixing other substances together

electricity   an energy supply that we get from wall sockets or batteries

environment the world around us

fuel   something that is burned to provide power

insulation   material that stops heat from escaping

mining   digging rocks, such as coal, from the ground

pollution   damage to the environment caused by harmful substances

power station a place where electricity is made

recharge   to give a battery more energy so that it can be used again

turbine   a machine that turns to make electricity

Index

Notes for parents and teachers

- Safety. Explain the dangers of electricity and electrical equipment, especially mains electricity. Make sure that rules about the use of switches and sockets are understood. Batteries are also dangerous and should not be handled too much. You could explain more about rechargeable batteries and the proper way to dispose of used batteries.

- Walking or cycling to school raises safety issues. Children should be taught that parents and teachers must be aware of what they are doing, and that children must never walk or cycle alone. When cycling, children should wear a safety helmet, reflective clothing, and fix lights to their bike.

- Children could learn more about the Sun and what it is—a huge, glowing ball of hot gases, like other stars. The Sun's rays travel at nearly 200,000 miles (300,000 kilometers) a second and take about eight minutes to reach Earth. Important: never look directly at the Sun. Its bright light could cause permanent damage to your eyes.

- Introduce and discuss other energy sources. Biomass—including the traditional burning of wood for cooking and heating—and geothermal power are other sources of renewable energy. Nuclear power—non-renewable because it depends on mined uranium.

- What did people do years ago, before the days of power stations and electricity? Look at how people used to wash and dry clothes, for example, using muscle power and energy from the wind and Sun.

- Talk about insulation and wrapping up warm. Fur, feathers, and wool are all good natural insulators, keeping the bodies of animals warm. Explain how insulation traps layers of air.

- Look through the book and talk about the pictures. Read the captions and then ask questions about other things in the photographs that have not been mentioned.